TESTIMONIALS

Veronica and Bernie are great to work with and have truly helped Surf Life Saving Australia communicate the exciting future ahead. Through this book, their knowledge and experience will help many leaders and future leaders who are looking to evolve the way that they work with their teams and the people around them. Well done!

Adam Weir
CEO, Surf Life Saving Australia

I have known Veronica for a number of years and have always maintained that she has absolute commitment to improve whatever she does. Again, this project with Bernie is exactly in that vein. This project will benefit many executives, managers and staff who are looking to improve the way they work with their people and staff. I look forward to seeing where this will lead to next! Well done, Veronica and Bernie. Project well done!

Dr Bruno D'Aprano PhD
Past President Pascoe Vale Rotary PHF
Ambassador, Australian Mental Health Foundation

This transformative guide offers purpose-driven leaders a powerful framework for navigating organisational evolution through the lens of "love-based" transformation rather than "fear-driven" management, providing practical pathways. True organisational re-founding requires conscious choice-making at critical crossroads, making this a valuable resource for leaders committed to creating sustainable impact in our rapidly changing world.

Gavin Clifford
Co-Founder and CEO, Ezy Chef Group

In our work helping brave businesses cut through in an increasingly distracted world, we see that the leaders who remain truly relevant are the ones willing to ask deeper questions. This book is an accessible and timely entry point into the kinds of conversations that matter.

David O'Loughlin
Chair and CEO, KWPX + Partners

This helpful guide is designed for leaders who want to make informed decisions. It uses stories and practical advice to show how choosing love over fear and possibility over limitation can transform lives. This book is essential for anyone ready to lead with confidence and a clear vision.

Dr Nuttawuth (Wuth) Muenjohn PhD, CMBE
Associate Professor in Management, University of Bradford
Head of Research, Global and Sustainable Business Futures (GSBF)

The path from reactive to proactive is not always clear. Bernie's concepts have helped my team and me Feed-forward to generate a rhythm that delivers on personal and business goals.

Glenn Hancock
Chief Operating Officer, Residential Care Bolton Clarke

I have always seen myself as a leader who makes connections and considers hearts and minds. The insights into purpose leadership have taken my leadership approach to a deeper level to aim to connect more meaningfully and with shared intent and understanding. As a leader, I'm often reminded that I will only know half of the reality. Colleagues toe the company line and might be passionate about some areas of the business but get on with other areas to keep life simple; but then they get agitated over time. I think others will really value the deeper practices of purpose leadership. There are skills we need to know and rehearse as leaders to be effective rather than transactional and to have real impact for ourselves and others.

Olly Jones
Chief Operating Officer, Healthcare Sector Member
Professional Development Organisation

This book moved me deeply by offering a powerful framework for thinking about transformation not only within organisations but also in us as leaders and change agents. What struck me most was the contrast between fear-based, managerial-led transformation and purpose-led, love-based transformation. The clarity with which these paradigms were articulated made me reflect on my own leadership choices and the environment I seek to create for others. In a time marked by uncertainty and rapid change, this message feels more urgent than ever. It reminds us that transformation is not just about strategy, but about mindset and that choosing to lead from a place of purpose, empathy and abundance can fundamentally alter the direction and impact of our work. I believe others will find value in recognising which stage of the transformation journey they are in, and how courage, co-creation, and discernment can lead to more meaningful and sustainable change.

Dr Sehrish Shahid
Lecturer Management, RMIT University

As someone who supports organisations through transformation and speaks on leadership, change and connection, I know how overwhelming it can feel when the path ahead is unclear. *For Purpose Leaders Navigating What Matters* offers both structure and flexibility.

Its blend of practical frameworks and a choose-your-own-adventure style makes it a grounded, adaptable guide for leaders at a turning point – inviting them to choose between leading through fear and control, or with heart, purpose and a drive to create lasting impact.

Michelle Letho
Strategic Sales and Partnerships Leader,
Speaker and Transformation Community Host

In today's rapidly changing world, this book highlights the importance of purpose-led leadership that's grounded in personal values and collective team journeys. Regardless of an organisation's size or stage of transformation, leaders' choices shape their future direction. Thanks Bernie and Vee for illustrating so well the diverse possibilities available to leaders who embrace purposeful leadership and choose purpose-led paths.

Dr Robert Lee PhD
Senior Healthcare Sector Executive,
Not-for-Profit Board Director

For Purpose Leaders Navigating What Matters

Which Path Will You Choose?

FOR PURPOSE LEADERS NAVIGATING WHAT MATTERS

Which Path Will You Choose?

BERNIE KELLY &
VERONICA HASLAM

Copyright © Bernie Kelly and Veronica Haslam 2025

All models copyright © Bernie Kelly and Veronica Haslam 2025

First published in 2025 by Bison Press

All rights reserved. No part of this publication may be reproduced by any means without the prior written consent of the publisher. Every effort has been made to trace (and seek permission for use of) the original source of material used within this book. Where the attempt has been unsuccessful, the publisher would be pleased to hear from the author / publisher to rectify any omission.

Typeset, printed and bound in Australia by BookPOD

ISBN: 978-1-7642216-0-3 (pbk) 978-1-7642216-1-0 (e-book)

A catalogue record for this book is available from the National Library of Australia

"The most important decision a purpose-led leader makes isn't about the route – it's about whether they choose to lead from management or purpose, from constraint or possibility, from fear or love."

PREFACE

We created this book to support leaders in lifting the conversation among their peers and teams. Lifting the conversation out of the specific details and tightly held perspectives to illuminate pathways that fulfil purpose.

Purpose Organisation leaders are faced with many conundrums. Conundrums are problems that cannot be solved from current perspectives. That's the definition of the word, and it's such a healthy reminder wherever industry leaders and experts gather.

Whether in the Boardroom, at the Exec table, or industry forums there are so many immediate issues and tactical opportunities that grab our attention. This will always be a part of it.

We know the stories here are fictional, and not as layered as your specific situation.

In our work along the path with Purpose leaders like you we know there's a lot more we need to do along the way.

It feels like a twist of irony this book and its simplified stories are for serving the wisest and convicted among us. People who have already navigated so much to be where they are today. We came to this book the long way. Obsessed with our own mission, wrestling with the purpose path beside leaders that continue to inspire and teach us, and taking on the signals of what is actually helpful.

We invite you to create the space to play along, follow the stories of Capella, Polaris, and Sirius and gather others to bring it back to what really matters for you.

Thank you for sharing the Purpose Leaders path in our world.

YOUR REFOUNDING JOURNEY

THE CARE-ECONOMIC CROSSROADS	**1**
Being at the Trailhead	5
The Two Paradigms: Which Path Will You Choose?	7
Understanding Your Refounding Stage	9
Meet the Three Leaders	13
Choose Your Leader's Journey	19
CHART YOUR PATH	**21**
REUNION: WHERE ALL REFOUNDING PATHS REGROUP	**105**
Cross-Stage Learning Insights	111
The Care-Economic Revolution: Your Choice	113
Your Next Steps: Continuing the Journey	115
Being Fit For Purpose: The Comprehensive Guide	117
The Trail Markers	119
A bit about Bernie & Vee	125
PurposeOrgOS™	127

THE CARE-ECONOMIC CROSSROADS

Capella reviewed the leadership development program participation rates with mixed feelings. Over 6,000 people across their 10,000+ aged care network had enrolled. Exactly what they'd hoped for when committing to progressive industry leadership. Yet feedback from the front lines told a different story: "We want to provide positive ageing experiences, but we're still operating like efficient care delivery machines rather than life-enhancement partners."

Two hundred miles away, Polaris sat in his food company's distribution warehouse, watching pallets of their purpose-driven products being loaded onto trucks bound for major retail outlets. Three years into scaling from his personal health transformation origin story into a $25 million operation, the path forward felt murkier than ever. The bold ambitions that had carried them through expansion now bumped against economic realities that demanded innovative approaches they hadn't yet discovered.

Meanwhile, Sirius stood at the edge of the community space her volunteer-based organisation had created, feeling simultaneously proud and conflicted. Their century-old heritage had evolved through multiple initiatives across different locations and eras, but recent government funding opportunities seemed to pull them further from their original purpose. How do you professionalise without losing the unique ethos that made your community-centred work valuable in the first place?

Three purpose-led leaders. Three different sectors. Three organisations at different stages of the same fundamental journey.

Each had inherited something precious: Capella, a network of organisations with over 100 years of combined history now unified under bold leadership development commitments; Polaris, a personal health transformation journey transformed into substantial market presence with powerful distribution relationships; and Sirius, a community-based legacy of member engagement that had survived generational shifts and cultural changes.

But each now faced a reality that their successful, substantial organisations needed to evolve – not because of immediate crisis, but because their current approaches might not be sufficient for the care-economic challenges ahead.

These weren't crisis-driven changes. These were conscious **refounding choices** that purpose-led organisations must make to remain relevant and impactful in a changing world.

"Every purpose-led organisation must navigate the choice between management and purpose, between constraint and possibility, between fear and love."

BEING AT THE TRAILHEAD

As morning light crept across the valley where these three leaders had gathered around a campfire, a weathered guide appeared. She moved with the quiet confidence of someone who had helped countless purpose-led organisations navigate transformation.

"I've been watching your preparations," she said, settling beside the dying embers. "Each of you stands at the same fundamental crossroads that every purpose-led organisation must navigate: **the choice between management and purpose, between constraint and possibility, between fear and love.**"

She gestured toward two paths leading from the valley.

"What many leaders don't realise is that this choice determines not just where you arrive, but who you become as an organisation capable of sustained transformation in the Care-Economic Revolution."

"At the heart of every purpose-led organisation's journey lies a profound choice between two fundamentally different ways of seeing and operating."

THE TWO PARADIGMS: WHICH PATH WILL YOU CHOOSE?

At the heart of every purpose-led organisation's journey lies a profound choice between two fundamentally different ways of seeing and operating:

The Managerial-Led Transformation (Fear-Based)

- **Fear-driven decisions** based on potential threats and risk aversion
- **Judgement-oriented** thinking that categorises situations as good/bad
- **Blame orientation** that attributes problems to external factors
- **Passive approach** that waits for others to solve problems
- **Focus on problems** and what can't be controlled
- **Short-term focus** prioritising immediate results over sustainable impact
- **Individual success** measured by personal achievements
- **Scarcity mindset** that hoards resources and operates from limitation

The Purpose-Led Transformation (Love-Based)

- **Purpose-driven decisions** rooted in values and meaningful contribution
- **Discernment-oriented** approach that seeks to understand before evaluating
- **Responsibility orientation** that focuses on creative response to challenges
- **Intentional co-creation** that actively shapes circumstances
- **Focus on opportunities** and expanding circles of influence
- **Balanced perspective** that serves both immediate needs and long-term vision
- **Impact beyond self** measured by collective contribution and ripple effects
- **Abundance mindset** that shares resources and creates generative possibilities

The guide looked at each leader in turn. "This choice manifests differently depending on where you are in your refounding journey, but it's the same essential choice. The paradigm you choose will determine not just your destination, but your capacity for navigating whatever terrain emerges."

UNDERSTANDING YOUR REFOUNDING STAGE

Before meeting our three leaders in depth, take a moment to identify where you are in your refounding journey:

Beginning Stage: Sensing the Need Recognition Phase – Building Courage for Change

This stage encompasses the dawning recognition that fundamental change is necessary – whether driven by external shifts, internal evolution, or new strategic intentions. Organisations find themselves at the threshold of transformation, sensing that their current approaches, structures, or ways of working may no longer be sufficient for the impact they're called to create.

The beginning stage often involves identifying new purposes or reimagining existing ones, recognising that stakeholder needs have evolved, or acknowledging that the organisation's potential exceeds its current capacity. Leaders may be grappling with how to honour institutional heritage whilst preparing for necessary adaptation. This phase requires building internal courage and consensus for change that hasn't yet been clearly defined.

Key Characteristics:

- Sensing disconnect between current capacity and desired impact

- Recognising shifting external landscapes or stakeholder expectations
- Identifying new strategic intentions requiring different approaches
- Building organisational readiness for undefined but necessary change
- Balancing respect for heritage with openness to transformation
- Creating space for emergence whilst maintaining operational stability

Mid-Cycle Stage: Actively Transforming Implementation Phase – Navigating Complex Change

This stage represents the active work of transformation – implementing new approaches, adapting structures, and evolving practices whilst maintaining organisational coherence and stakeholder confidence. Organisations are managing the complexity of change across multiple dimensions simultaneously: operational, cultural, strategic, and relational.

Mid-cycle transformation involves navigating resource constraints, managing competing priorities, and sustaining momentum through inevitable setbacks. Leaders must balance the urgency of change with the patience required for deep transformation, often whilst maintaining service delivery and stakeholder relationships. This phase tests organisational resilience and adaptability.

Key Characteristics:

- Managing multiple simultaneous changes across different organisational levels
- Balancing transformation work with ongoing operational demands
- Navigating resource allocation between current needs and future capacity
- Maintaining stakeholder confidence during periods of uncertainty
- Adapting governance and decision-making processes for increased complexity
- Building new capabilities whilst preserving essential organisational strengths
- Measuring progress when traditional metrics may not capture transformation

Renewing/Redefining Stage: Deepening Impact Evolution Phase – Expanding Influence

This stage involves refining and deepening the changes implemented, whilst exploring how transformation enables expanded influence and impact. Organisations are integrating new ways of working into their identity, culture, and external relationships. The focus shifts from managing change to leveraging transformation for greater purpose fulfilment.

Renewal may involve expanding reach, deepening relationships, or evolving the organisation's role within broader ecosystems. Leaders are often navigating questions of growth, sustainability, and legacy whilst ensuring that evolution strengthens rather than dilutes organisational purpose. This phase requires sophisticated balance between stability and continued adaptation.

Key Characteristics:

- Integrating transformational changes into organisational identity and culture
- Exploring expanded influence and deeper impact opportunities
- Managing growth whilst preserving essential organisational characteristics
- Navigating complex stakeholder relationships and competing expectations
- Preparing for succession and institutional continuity
- Balancing innovation with consolidation of successful changes
- Defining and communicating evolved purpose and impact to diverse audiences
- Creating sustainable models for continued adaptation and growth

If you'd like to find where you are currently at, check out the Free Trek Readiness Assessment at:

www.PurposeOrgOS.com/freediagnostic

MEET THE THREE LEADERS

Capella – Aged Care Network Leader (Beginning Stage)

Capella leads a network of over 10,000 people across multiple aged care facilities that represent the consolidation of organisations with heritage spanning over 100 years. They've made a significant commitment to leadership development with 6,000 people in their leadership pathways, positioning themselves to lead industry transformation toward more progressive approaches.

The recognition moment came during a leadership development session when a seasoned care manager shared: "We've got solid operational foundations, and I appreciate the investment in our development. But I keep thinking about how care has changed – residents are with us for six to twelve months now, not years like before. We're providing sub-acute clinical care, not long-term residential community. How do we honour our century of caring wisdom whilst becoming excellent at this very different role?"

This captured the complexity Capella faces. Their network had been built around different heritage approaches to aged care. The regulatory environment demands clinical excellence they're still developing capacity for. Community expectations have shifted dramatically following sector scrutiny. The funding models don't match the actual care intensity required. Yet they're committed to being industry leaders rather than followers.

Recent consolidation brought together different legacy computer systems, operating procedures, and leadership styles. Some locations had been operating for 100+ years, others for 20–30 years. The integration challenge is substantial, but so is the opportunity to create something that transcends what any individual organisation could achieve.

Capella stands at the **beginning of recognising** that refounding their unified network will require more than operational integration – it demands evolution into clinical excellence that maintains their heritage of dignified, relationship-centred care.

Capella's Paradigm Choice:

- **Managerial-Led Transformation Path:** Focus on proving that relationship-centred care can meet contemporary standards
- **Purpose-Led Transformation Path:** Integrate heritage wisdom with clinical excellence to pioneer positive ageing approaches that exceed traditional and regulatory expectations

Polaris – Purpose-Driven Food Company Leader (Mid-Cycle Stage)

Polaris co-founded a purpose-driven food company rooted in his personal health transformation following a Type 2 diabetes diagnosis, growing it to target $25 million revenue with powerful distribution relationships in place. Their purpose extends beyond profit into health and wellness sectors, built on values of supplier respect and integrity that reflect his personal health journey.

The challenge intensified when economic conditions created a "hard patch" that revealed limitations in their current approach. While they'd achieved significant scale and established excellent distribution partnerships, the pathway to their bold ambitions requires innovative approaches they haven't yet discovered. The road has proven more difficult than they'd fully comprehended initially.

Polaris recognises he's in succession-thinking mode, needing to create pathways for future leaders to take the organisation where it needs to go whilst maintaining the purpose authenticity that defines them. The question isn't whether they can continue – it's whether they can evolve approaches that honour their foundation story whilst achieving the scale needed for sustainable impact.

Their distributor relationships represent significant assets, but maximising these requires operational innovations that stretch current capabilities. The purpose-driven market positioning is strong, but economic pressures demand efficiency improvements that could potentially compromise the integrity-based approaches that built their reputation.

Polaris is **mid-cycle in active transformation**, knowing they've done excellent foundational work whilst recognising they need to develop successor leadership and innovative approaches for the journey ahead.

Polaris's Paradigm Choice:

- **Managerial-Led Transformation Path:** Focus on operational efficiency and cost management to weather economic challenges
- **Purpose-Led Transformation Path:** Use economic pressure as catalyst for innovations that strengthen both purpose authenticity and market effectiveness

Sirius – Community-Based Member Organisation Leader (Renewing/Redefining Stage)

Sirius leads a volunteer-based, member organisation with federated structure that has built heritage through multiple community-serving initiatives across different locations and eras. They carry many strands of different programs, some of which may now be legacy rather than core competence, whilst navigating changing expectations about professionalisation and government partnerships.

The evolution question crystallised when major government funding opportunities emerged that could significantly expand their community impact. However, these opportunities come with standardisation requirements that might compromise the localised autonomy and unique ethos that has attracted members and volunteers for generations. The risk of becoming too dependent on one funding source conflicts with their community-centred independence.

Recent years have brought generational changes in what members seek from their organisation. Traditional meaning-making approaches don't resonate with newer demographics, yet professionalisation efforts risk losing the authentic community connection that differentiates their work from government services. They operate under increasing regulatory and safety requirements that force standardisation, potentially at the expense of the flexible, responsive approaches that built their community relationships.

The organisation has accepted new expectations and funding from sources that may not align perfectly with their original purpose. When resources are limited, choices must be made about which initiatives to maintain, potentially compromising the breadth of community connection that has been their strength.

Sirius is in the **renewing/redefining stage**, needing to reimagine how their heritage of community engagement can evolve for contemporary relevance whilst maintaining the authentic relationships that make their work uniquely valuable.

Sirius's Paradigm Choice:

- **Managerial-Led Transformation Path:** Professionalise operations and accept government funding with accompanying standardisation requirements
- **Purpose-Led Transformation Path:** Innovate approaches that strengthen both professional excellence and authentic community connection whilst maintaining funding independence

CHOOSE YOUR LEADER'S JOURNEY

Which leader's refounding stage and sector most closely matches your current organisational situation?

Follow Capella's Journey (Beginning Stage) if you:

- Lead a substantial organisation in aged care, healthcare, or community services
- Have recently consolidated multiple entities or approaches under unified leadership
- Are committed to industry leadership but recognise current approaches need evolution
- Need to integrate different heritage systems whilst building progressive capability
- ➡ *Go to **Section Capella-1** (page 23)*

Follow Polaris's Journey (Mid-Cycle Stage) if you:

- Lead a purpose-driven organisation in social enterprise, food/agriculture, or mission-driven business
- Have achieved significant scale but face economic conditions requiring innovation
- Are in succession-thinking phase whilst maintaining founder authenticity

- Need to develop new approaches whilst strengthening existing market relationships

➡ *Go to **Section Polaris-1** (page 28)*

Follow Sirius's Journey (Renewing/Redefining Stage) if you:

- Lead a community-based organisation in member services, community development, or volunteer coordination
- Navigate tensions between professionalisation and authentic community connection
- Manage funding opportunities that might compromise mission independence
- Need to evolve member engagement for contemporary relevance whilst honouring heritage

➡ *Go to **Section Sirius-1** (page 33)*

CHART YOUR PATH

"Each organisation brought not just different systems and procedures, but fundamentally different philosophies."

CAPELLA-1

The Heritage Integration Moment (Beginning Stage)

Capella had been reflecting on more than just the leadership development feedback. The consolidation of their network had revealed something she hadn't fully anticipated: each organisation brought not just different systems and procedures, but fundamentally different philosophies about what excellent aged care meant in contemporary contexts.

"We've successfully brought together organisations with over 100 years of combined heritage," she told her executive team. "But I'm realising that operational integration isn't sufficient. We're trying to lead industry transformation whilst still operating from models designed for when people lived in care for years, not months. How do we honour our heritage wisdom whilst becoming excellent at clinical care that didn't exist when our founders started this work?"

The challenge wasn't their commitment to dignity and relationship – it was that their inherited approaches weren't designed for the clinical intensity of contemporary aged care. Residents now arrive requiring hospital-level nursing support within family-atmosphere environments. Regulatory requirements demand documentation that seems to pull staff away from relationship time. The funding models assume efficiency ratios that don't match the actual care complexity.

Her executive team offered three different perspectives:

Operations Director: "Our heritage is our strength, and the sector has over-corrected toward clinical models that lose the human element. We should focus on proving that relationship-centred care can meet contemporary standards without losing what makes us special."

Clinical Services Manager: "I appreciate our heritage, but we need to acknowledge that clinical excellence is now essential for dignified care. Maybe we can integrate heritage values with clinical innovation rather than seeing them as competing priorities."

Leadership Development Coordinator: "What if this consolidation is creating opportunity for something unprecedented. Organisations that excel at both clinical care and relationship-centred approaches? Our heritage becomes foundation for innovation rather than constraint on evolution."

 THE PARADIGM CHOICE

Managerial-driven decisions focus on protecting against threats rather than creating toward possibilities

Purpose-led leadership lifts both the leader and possibilities of what you serve

FOR PURPOSE LEADERS NAVIGATING WHAT MATTERS

Insightful Pause Practice.

Before making any major path choice.

Take a moment to step back from the immediate decision and connect with your deeper leadership wisdom.

What is really happening here?

What does this mean for what matters most?

What wants to emerge through this choice?

How might this choice create ripples beyond what I can see?

_____

_____

_____

BERNIE KELLY AND VERONICA HASLAM

As Capella (Beginning Stage), how do you respond to this heritage integration moment?

A. Focus on proving that relationship-centred care can meet contemporary standards: "Our heritage approach is still the right foundation. We need to demonstrate its continued relevance."

➡ *Go to **Section Capella-2A** (page 38)*

B. Integrate heritage values with clinical excellence through strategic planning: "We need systematic approaches to combining our legacy strengths with contemporary requirements."

➡ *Go to **Section Capella-2B** (page 43)*

C. Embrace heritage as foundation for clinical innovation: "What if our century of caring wisdom becomes the platform for pioneering approaches that exceed both traditional and regulatory expectations?"

➡ *Go to **Section Capella-2C** (page 48)*

POLARIS-1

The Innovation Imperative (Mid-Cycle Stage)

Polaris stared at the quarterly financials, feeling both frustrated and determined. Their revenue was solid, their distribution relationships were stronger than ever, and their purpose-driven positioning resonated with customers who cared about integrity and social impact. Yet the numbers revealed what he'd been sensing for months: their current approaches weren't sufficient for the economic conditions and growth ambitions ahead.

"We've built something meaningful," he told his co-founder and leadership team. "My health transformation journey became a company that serves thousands of people facing similar dietary challenges. We've got distribution partnerships that other companies spend years trying to develop. But I'm realising that good intentions and strong relationships aren't enough for the innovation this next phase requires."

The challenge wasn't their purpose authenticity or market positioning – it was that scaling their impact required operational excellence and efficiency innovations they hadn't yet developed. The economic headwinds were revealing gaps between their values-driven foundation and their business execution capabilities.

His leadership team offered three different perspectives:

Operations Manager: "We need to focus on efficiency improvements and cost management to weather these economic conditions. Maybe we can revisit expansion plans once we've stabilised our current operations."

Sales & Distribution Director: "Our distributor relationships are incredible assets that we're not maximising. Maybe we need to invest in operational innovations that help us take better advantage of these partnerships while maintaining our integrity standards."

Co-founder/Purpose Guardian: "What if this economic pressure is exactly what we need to develop the innovations that will make us sustainable long-term? What if these constraints are pushing us toward approaches that strengthen both our purpose authenticity and our business effectiveness?"

 KNOW • FOCUS • BE

KNOW what matters: Without connection to deeper purpose, efficiency becomes empty activity

FOCUS what matters: Trying to serve two paradigms simultaneously serves neither effectively

BE what matters: Purpose-led leadership lifts both the leader and possibilities of what you serve

Insightful Pause Practice.

Before making any major path choice.

Take a moment to step back from the immediate decision and connect with your deeper leadership wisdom.

What is really happening here?

What does this mean for what matters most?

What wants to emerge through this choice?

How might this choice create ripples beyond what I can see?

_____

_____

_____

FOR PURPOSE LEADERS NAVIGATING WHAT MATTERS

As Polaris (Mid-Cycle Stage), how do you respond to this innovation imperative?

    A. Focus on efficiency improvements and cost management: "We need to stabilise current operations before pursuing expansion ambitions."

➡ *Go to **Section Polaris-2A** (page 53)*

    B. Invest strategically in operational innovations while maintaining purpose standards: "We need systematic approaches to maximising our distribution assets whilst preserving our integrity foundation."

➡ *Go to **Section Polaris-2B** (page 58)*

    C. Use economic pressure as catalyst for purpose-driven innovations: "What if these constraints are calling us to develop approaches that make purpose and profit mutually reinforcing?"

➡ *Go to **Section Polaris-2C** (page 63)*

SIRIUS-1

The Authenticity Evolution Question (Renewing/Redefining Stage)

Sirius sat in the community centre that had hosted their organisation's activities for over three decades, surrounded by thank-you letters, photos from community events, and the latest government funding opportunity documents. The contrast was striking: evidence of decades of meaningful community connection alongside partnership possibilities that could dramatically expand their impact – if they were willing to accept the accompanying requirements.

"We've maintained authentic community relationships through generational changes and cultural shifts that ended many similar organisations," she told her volunteer board. "We've adapted our approaches whilst preserving the essence of what makes our work valuable. But I'm wondering if this government funding opportunity is asking us to choose between growth and authenticity in ways we haven't faced before."

The challenge wasn't their community connection or their adaptive capacity – it was that the professionalisation and standardisation requirements seemed designed for organisations that operated like government services rather than community-rooted member organisations. The funding could expand their impact significantly, but the reporting requirements and operational standards might compromise the flexible, responsive approaches that had built their community relationships.

Her board offered three different perspectives:

Long-serving Community Representative: "We've survived this long because we stayed true to our community-first approach. Maybe we should focus on sustainable growth that doesn't compromise what makes us different from government services."

Newer Board Member (Grant Writing Experience): "Professional standards and community authenticity don't have to be opposing forces. Maybe we can develop approaches that satisfy funding requirements whilst strengthening rather than compromising our community connections."

Member Services Coordinator: "What if this funding opportunity is actually calling us to pioneer approaches that prove community authenticity and professional excellence can be mutually reinforcing? What if we're being asked to evolve our model rather than choose between our heritage and our growth?"

 THE THREE-PHASE JOURNEY

CLARIFY YOUR PATH: Start from purpose and abundance, not problems and scarcity

BE FIT FOR YOUR PATH: Develop integrated wisdom across Being, Feeling, Thinking, and Doing

LIFT YOUR VANTAGE POINT: Purpose-led leadership kindles the spark in others

FOR PURPOSE LEADERS NAVIGATING WHAT MATTERS

Insightful Pause Practice.

Before making any major path choice.

Take a moment to step back from the immediate decision and connect with your deeper leadership wisdom.

What is really happening here?

What does this mean for what matters most?

What wants to emerge through this choice?

How might this choice create ripples beyond what I can see?

_____

_____

_____

BERNIE KELLY AND VERONICA HASLAM

As Sirius (Renewing/Redefining Stage), how do you respond to this authenticity evolution question?

    A. Focus on sustainable growth that preserves community-first approaches: "We should expand in ways that don't require us to operate like government services."

➡ *Go to **Section Sirius-2A** (page 68)*

    B. Develop strategic approaches that satisfy funding requirements whilst maintaining community connection: "We need systematic ways to meet professional standards without compromising our relationships."

➡ *Go to **Section Sirius-2B** (page 73)*

    C. Pioneer integration of community authenticity with professional excellence: "What if this opportunity is calling us to prove these approaches can strengthen each other?"

➡ *Go to **Section Sirius-2C** (page 78)*

CAPELLA-2A

The Heritage Protection Path (Beginning Stage)

Capella chose to focus on proving that relationship-centred care could meet contemporary standards without fundamental evolution. She worked with her operations team to document their heritage approaches, create training programs that emphasised their century of caring wisdom, and develop communication strategies that highlighted the human elements that distinguished their network from more clinical competitors.

The results were positive in the short term. Staff appreciated feeling more connected to their heritage identity, and families choosing their facilities often mentioned the "family atmosphere" that set them apart from institutional alternatives. The leadership development program gained momentum as people felt proud of their distinctive approach to aged care.

But eighteen months later, Capella realised that emphasising heritage without evolving capability hadn't addressed the underlying challenge. Residents were still arriving with clinical needs that required hospital-level expertise within community-atmosphere environments. Staff still felt torn between relationship time and documentation requirements. The funding models still didn't match the actual intensity of care required.

More concerning, several key clinical staff had left for organisations that were innovating approaches to integrate relationship excellence with clinical expertise. The sector was evolving around them while they focused on preserving rather than advancing their approaches.

> **YOUR CHOICE DETERMINES YOUR DESTINATION**
>
> *The Managerial-led Paradigm will make you efficient at managing decline*
>
> *Purpose-led leadership lifts both the leader and possibilities of what you serve*
>
> **Which path will you choose?**

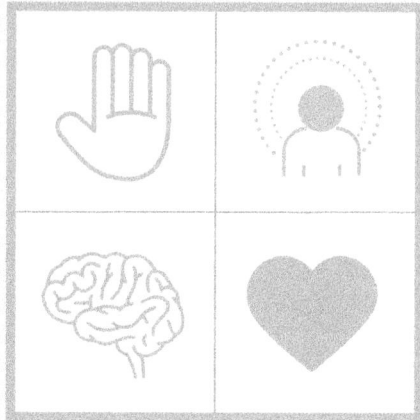

Insightful Pause Practice.

When recognising your current path may need adjustment.

Pause and notice what this realisation is revealing.

What else is this moment showing me?

How do I stay aligned with my deeper purpose?

What is being asked of me here?

_____

_____

_____

_____

FOR PURPOSE LEADERS NAVIGATING WHAT MATTERS

Capella realises that heritage protection without capability evolution hasn't addressed the fundamental challenges facing contemporary aged care.

How does Capella respond to this realisation?

A. Accept that heritage preservation is sufficient: "We've maintained what makes us special. The sector can evolve around us while we stay true to our foundations."

➡ *Go to **Section Capella – Vantage Point Review – A** (page 93)*

B. Recognise that heritage innovation may be necessary after all: "Maybe we need to honour our heritage by evolving it rather than just preserving it."

➡ *Go to **Section Capella-3C** (page 81)*

CAPELLA-2B

The Strategic Integration Path (Beginning Stage)

Capella chose to integrate heritage values with clinical excellence through systematic strategic planning. She worked with her executive team to develop a phased approach that would honour their century of caring wisdom whilst building the clinical capabilities needed for contemporary aged care.

The approach felt both ambitious and manageable. They created heritage-clinical integration committees that included long-serving staff and new clinical specialists. They developed training programmes that taught clinical protocols through the lens of relationship-centred care. They implemented pilot programmes at select facilities to test integrated approaches before network-wide rollout.

The strategic integration produced measurable progress across multiple indicators. Staff appreciated the structured approach that honoured their experience whilst developing new capabilities. Families noticed improvements in both clinical outcomes and relationship quality. Regulatory compliance improved without sacrificing the personal touch that distinguished their network.

But eighteen months later, Capella began noticing concerning patterns. While they had successfully implemented integrated systems, the transformation felt more mechanical than transformational. Staff were following new protocols effectively, but the innovative spirit that could have made them industry pioneers was constrained by the systematic, measured approach they had chosen.

More troubling, the pace of change in the aged care sector was accelerating around them. Other organisations that had embraced more radical integration approaches were achieving breakthrough results that positioned them as sector leaders, while Capella's network was achieving competent improvement but not industry transformation.

 THE PARADIGM CHOICE

Managerial-driven decisions focus on protecting against threats rather than creating toward possibilities

Purpose-led leadership lifts both the leader and possibilities of what you serve

FOR PURPOSE LEADERS NAVIGATING WHAT MATTERS

Insightful Pause Practice.

When recognising your current path may need adjustment.

Pause and notice what this realisation is revealing.

What else is this moment showing me?

How do I stay aligned with my deeper purpose?

What is being asked of me here?

_____

_____

_____

_____

_____

BERNIE KELLY AND VERONICA HASLAM

Capella realises that systematic integration has produced improvement but may have limited the breakthrough innovation their consolidation could have enabled.

How does Capella respond to this realisation?

A. Accept that systematic improvement represents sufficient progress: "We've successfully integrated heritage and clinical excellence. Sometimes steady improvement is more sustainable than breakthrough innovation."

➡ *Go to **Section Capella – Vantage Point – B** (page 95)*

B. Recognise that their network may be ready for more transformational approaches: "Maybe our successful integration has created the foundation for the breakthrough innovation we initially held back from pursuing."

➡ *Go to **Section Capella-3C** (page 81)*

CAPELLA-2C

The Purpose-Led Transformation Path (Beginning Stage)

When Capella embraced heritage as foundation for clinical innovation, she shifted from asking "How do we preserve what we've always done?" to "How does our century of caring wisdom inform approaches that exceed contemporary expectations?" She convened innovation teams that included both long-serving heritage keepers and clinical excellence champions.

"Our heritage isn't something to protect from change," she told her network leadership. "It's wisdom that can inform breakthrough approaches to clinical care that other organisations can't achieve because they don't have our foundation of relationship expertise."

The breakthrough came when their most experienced care manager observed: "We've always known that healing happens in relationship, not just through medical procedures. What if we design clinical protocols that strengthen relationships rather than replacing them? What if our century of caring experience becomes our advantage in creating clinical excellence that feels more human, not less?"

This reframe opened revolutionary possibilities. Instead of seeing clinical requirements and relationship care as competing priorities, they began pioneering "relationship-informed clinical excellence" – approaches that used their heritage wisdom to create clinical care that was more effective because it was more relational.

The innovation felt both challenging and natural – challenging because it required developing new capabilities, natural because it honoured the caring instincts that had drawn people to their work originally.

> **THE WISDOM CAPACITIES INTEGRATION**
>
> *BEING: Stay connected to authentic purpose and presence*
>
> *FEELING: Navigate with emotional intelligence and relationship wisdom*
>
> *THINKING: Expand mental models beyond either/or to both/and possibilities*
>
> *DOING: Take action aligned with purpose, building sustainable practices*

Insightful Pause Practice.

When recognising your current path may need adjustment.

Pause and notice what this realisation is revealing.

What else is this moment showing me?

How do I stay aligned with my deeper purpose?

What is being asked of me here?

_____

_____

_____

_____

FOR PURPOSE LEADERS NAVIGATING WHAT MATTERS

This approach required developing what Capella learned to call "Being Fit For Purpose" – the capacity to honour heritage whilst pioneering innovation, to serve both clinical excellence and relationship depth simultaneously.

Capella 's refounding journey continues:

➡ *Go to **Section Capella – PURPOSE – Vantage Point Review** (page 87)*

POLARIS-2A

The Stability Focus Path (Mid-Cycle Stage)

Polaris decided to focus on efficiency improvements and cost management to weather the economic conditions before pursuing growth ambitions. He worked with his operations manager to identify cost-saving opportunities, streamline production processes, and defer expansion plans until their financial foundation was more secure.

The approach provided immediate relief. Cash flow improved, operational stress decreased, and the leadership team felt more confident about navigating economic uncertainty. Their distributor relationships remained strong, and customers continued appreciating their purpose-driven products.

The stabilisation phase produced measurable improvements in efficiency metrics and cost control. Polaris felt proud that they had navigated economic challenges without compromising their core values or laying off team members. The company achieved the financial stability they had been seeking.

But two years later, Polaris began noticing troubling patterns. While they had become more efficient at current operations, they hadn't developed the innovations needed for sustainable growth. Several competitors had used similar economic pressures as catalysts for breakthrough approaches that were now capturing market share. Their distributor partners were beginning to ask about new products and expanded offerings that Polaris's company wasn't prepared to deliver.

Most concerning, several of their most innovative team members had left for organisations where they could pioneer new approaches rather than optimise existing ones. The creative energy that had built their company was now focused on efficiency rather than evolution.

 THE PARADIGM CHOICE

Managerial-driven decisions focus on protecting against threats rather than creating toward possibilities

Purpose-led leadership lifts both the leader and possibilities of what you serve

FOR PURPOSE LEADERS NAVIGATING WHAT MATTERS

Insightful Pause Practice.

When recognising your current path may need adjustment.

Pause and notice what this realisation is revealing.

What else is this moment showing me?

How do I stay aligned with my deeper purpose?

What is being asked of me here?

_____

_____

_____

_____

Polaris realises that focusing on stability without innovation may have preserved current operations while limiting future possibilities.

How does Polaris respond to this realisation?

> **A.** Accept that operational stability represents sufficient achievement: "We've preserved our company and values through challenging times. Maybe sustainable growth isn't realistic in current conditions."

➡ *Go to **Section Polaris – Vantage Point Review – A** (page 97)*

> **B.** Recognise that innovation may be necessary for long-term sustainability: "Maybe economic pressure was pointing toward evolution we still need to pursue."

➡ *Go to **Section Polaris-3C** (page 83)*

POLARIS-2B

The Strategic Innovation Path (Mid-Cycle Stage)

Polaris chose to invest strategically in operational innovations whilst maintaining their purpose standards. He worked with his leadership team to identify specific areas where enhanced efficiency could strengthen rather than compromise their integrity-based approach, focusing on innovations that would maximise their distribution relationships whilst preserving their authentic foundation.

The approach felt both practical and principled. They invested in technology that improved production efficiency without compromising product quality. They developed new products that leveraged their distribution partnerships whilst staying true to his health transformation story. They hired specialists who could help them scale their operations without losing their purpose authenticity.

The strategic innovation produced positive results across key metrics. Operational efficiency improved, enabling them to serve more families whilst maintaining quality standards. Their distributors appreciated the enhanced product range and reliability. The leadership team felt confident they were building sustainable growth whilst preserving their core values.

But two years later, Polaris began questioning whether strategic innovation had been sufficient for the challenges they faced. While they had improved their current operations, they hadn't developed the breakthrough approaches that could have differentiated them significantly from competitors. The economic conditions that had prompted their innovation were improving, but other companies had used similar pressures to develop more transformational approaches.

Most concerning, their most creative team members were expressing restlessness with incremental innovation. They had joined a purpose-driven company expecting to pioneer new approaches to conscious commerce, but found themselves implementing systematic improvements to existing operations.

 KNOW • FOCUS • BE

KNOW what matters: Without connection to deeper purpose, efficiency becomes empty activity

FOCUS what matters: Trying to serve two paradigms simultaneously serves neither effectively

BE what matters: Purpose-led leadership lifts both the leader and possibilities of what you serve

Insightful Pause Practice.

When recognising your current path may need adjustment.

Pause and notice what this realisation is revealing.

What else is this moment showing me?

How do I stay aligned with my deeper purpose?

What is being asked of me here?

_____

_____

_____

_____

FOR PURPOSE LEADERS NAVIGATING WHAT MATTERS

Polaris realises that strategic innovation has produced operational improvements but may have constrained the transformational potential their purpose foundation could have supported.

How does Polaris respond to this realisation?

> **A.** Accept that strategic improvement represents realistic progress: "We've enhanced our operations whilst maintaining our values. Sometimes practical innovation is more sustainable than transformational risk-taking."

➡ *Go to **Section Polaris – Vantage Point Review – B** (page 99)*

> **B.** Recognise that their foundation may be ready for more transformational innovation: "Maybe our operational improvements have created the platform for the breakthrough approaches we initially considered too risky."

➡ *Go to **Section Polaris-3C** (page 83)*

POLARIS-2C

The Purpose-Led Transformation Path (Mid-Cycle Stage)

When Polaris chose to use economic pressure as catalyst for purpose-driven innovations, he reframed their financial challenges from obstacles to overcome to information about what their next evolution required. He gathered his team for strategic sessions focused on "What innovations would make purpose and profit mutually reinforcing?"

"These economic conditions aren't just testing our current business model," he told his leadership team. "They're revealing opportunities for approaches that could make us more sustainable and more impactful simultaneously. What if our purpose authenticity becomes our competitive advantage rather than a constraint on growth?"

The breakthrough came when their sales director observed: "Our distributor relationships give us access to markets that purpose-driven competitors spend years trying to reach. What if we develop products and approaches that help our distributors serve conscious consumers more effectively? What if his health transformation story becomes the foundation for innovations that serve people with similar health challenges at much greater scale?"

This insight led to a fundamental evolution of their business model. Instead of just producing purpose-driven products, they began pioneering "conscious commerce approaches" that helped distributors connect values-driven consumers with authentic social impact offerings.

The innovation required both maintaining their authentic foundation and developing sophisticated business capabilities they hadn't previously needed.

> **KNOW • FOCUS • BE**
>
> *KNOW what matters: Without connection to deeper purpose, efficiency becomes empty activity*
>
> *FOCUS what matters: Trying to serve two paradigms simultaneously serves neither effectively*
>
> *BE what matters: Purpose-led leadership lifts both the leader and possibilities of what you serve*

FOR PURPOSE LEADERS NAVIGATING WHAT MATTERS

Insightful Pause Practice.

When recognising your current path may need adjustment.

Pause and notice what this realisation is revealing.

What else is this moment showing me?

How do I stay aligned with my deeper purpose?

What is being asked of me here?

_____

_____

_____

_____

This approach required developing what Polaris learned to call "Being Fit For Purpose" – the capacity to use constraints as catalysts for innovation, to serve both authentic purpose and sustainable growth simultaneously.

Polaris's refounding journey continues:

➡ *Go to* **Section Polaris – PURPOSE alignment – Vantage Point review** *(page 89)*

SIRIUS-2A

The Community-First Path (Renewing/Redefining Stage)

Sirius decided to focus on sustainable growth that preserved their community-first approaches rather than accepting government funding with standardisation requirements. She worked with her board to identify alternative funding sources, develop fee-for-service offerings that aligned with their values, and create growth strategies that maintained their authentic community connections.

The approach felt principled and sustainable. They maintained their operational flexibility, preserved the localised autonomy that members valued, and avoided the dependency risks associated with major government funding. Their authentic community relationships continued deepening, and they attracted new members who appreciated their independence from bureaucratic constraints.

The community-first focus produced meaningful outcomes. Member satisfaction remained high, volunteer engagement was strong, and their organisation maintained the unique character that distinguished their work from government services. Sirius felt proud that they had grown whilst staying true to their foundational values.

But three years later, Sirius began noticing limiting patterns. While they had preserved their authentic community connections, they hadn't developed the professional capabilities that could have amplified their impact significantly. Other community organisations that had accepted similar government partnerships were now serving much larger populations with resources that Sirius 's organisation couldn't access independently.

More troubling, some community members were expressing frustration that services they needed were only available through more bureaucratic government program rather than the responsive, relationship-based approaches they preferred. The community authenticity they had preserved was becoming a limitation on their capacity to serve community needs.

 THE THREE-PHASE JOURNEY

CLARIFY YOUR PATH: Start from purpose and abundance, not problems and scarcity

BE FIT FOR YOUR PATH: Develop integrated wisdom across Being, Feeling, Thinking, and Doing

LIFT YOUR VANTAGE POINT: Purpose-led leadership kindles the spark in others

Insightful Pause Practice.

When recognising your current path may need adjustment.

Pause and notice what this realisation is revealing.

What else is this moment showing me?

How do I stay aligned with my deeper purpose?

What is being asked of me here?

_____

_____

_____

_____

FOR PURPOSE LEADERS NAVIGATING WHAT MATTERS

Sirius realises that preserving community authenticity without expanding professional capability may have limited their service impact.

How does Sirius respond to this realisation?

    A. Accept that community-first approaches represent sufficient contribution: "We've maintained authentic relationships that other organisations have lost. Our role is being genuinely community-centred rather than broadly impactful."

➡ *Go to **Section Sirius – Vantage Point Review – A** (page 91)*

    B. Recognise that professional development might enhance rather than compromise community connection: "Maybe we can serve our community better by developing capabilities we haven't yet explored."

➡ *Go to **Section Sirius-3C** (page 85)*

SIRIUS-2B

The Strategic Partnership Path (Renewing/Redefining Stage)

Sirius chose to develop strategic approaches that would satisfy funding requirements whilst maintaining community connection. She worked with her board to create structured approaches for engaging with government partnerships that would enhance their professional capabilities without compromising their authentic community relationships.

The approach felt both progressive and protective. They developed community consultation processes that ensured government funding supported community-designed programmes. They created professional development pathways that strengthened staff capabilities whilst preserving the responsive, relationship-based approaches that members valued. They established governance structures that maintained community voice whilst meeting regulatory requirements.

The strategic partnership approach produced meaningful improvements across multiple areas. They secured significant government funding that expanded their service capacity. Their staff developed enhanced professional skills that improved service quality. Their community maintained strong satisfaction with the responsive support they received.

But three years later, Sirius began noticing limitations in the strategic approach they had chosen. While they had successfully balanced community authenticity with professional standards, they hadn't achieved the transformational integration that could have made them a model for other community organisations. Their approach was working well, but it wasn't creating the breakthrough innovation that could influence sector development.

More troubling, other community organisations were pioneering more integrated approaches that were gaining recognition as models for community-professional excellence. Their strategic balance was maintaining their unique character, but it wasn't positioning them as leaders in community development innovation.

 THE THREE-PHASE JOURNEY

CLARIFY YOUR PATH: Start from purpose and abundance, not problems and scarcity

BE FIT FOR YOUR PATH: Develop integrated wisdom across Being, Feeling, Thinking, and Doing

LIFT YOUR VANTAGE POINT: Purpose-led leadership kindles the spark in others

FOR PURPOSE LEADERS NAVIGATING WHAT MATTERS

Insightful Pause Practice.

When recognising your current path may need adjustment.

Pause and notice what this realisation is revealing.

What else is this moment showing me?

How do I stay aligned with my deeper purpose?

What is being asked of me here?

_____

_____

_____

_____

_____

Sirius realises that strategic partnership has enhanced their capabilities but may have limited the transformational potential their community foundation could have supported.

How does Sirius respond to this realisation?

> **A.** Accept that strategic balance represents sustainable progress: "We've successfully maintained community authenticity whilst developing professional capabilities. Sometimes steady evolution is more sustainable than transformational innovation."

➡ *Go to **Section Sirius – Vantage Point Review – B** (page 103)*

> **B.** Recognise that their foundation may be ready for more transformational integration: "Maybe our successful balance has created the platform for the breakthrough community-professional integration we initially considered too ambitious."

➡ *Go to **Section SIRIUS-3C** (page 85)*

SIRIUS-2C

The Purpose-Led Transformation Path (Renewing/Redefining Stage)

When Sirius chose to pioneer integration of community authenticity with professional excellence, she reframed the funding opportunity from a choice between growth and authenticity to an innovation challenge: "How do we develop professional approaches that strengthen rather than compromise our community connections?"

She convened working groups that included long-serving community members, newer volunteers with professional expertise, and potential government partners to explore this question: "What would professional standards look like that enhance rather than replace the responsive, relationship-based approaches our community values?"

The breakthrough came when one of their most respected community elders observed: "Professional doesn't have to mean bureaucratic. What if these standards help us serve our community more effectively while teaching government program how community-centred work actually operates? What if we become the bridge between authentic community connection and professional excellence that both sectors need?"

This insight led to a fundamental evolution of their organisational model. Instead of choosing between community authenticity and professional capability, they began pioneering "community-informed professional excellence" – approaches that met funding requirements whilst strengthening community relationships.

The innovation felt both risky and exciting – risky because it required developing capabilities they'd never needed, exciting because it could amplify their community impact in ways they'd never imagined possible.

> **THE WISDOM CAPACITIES INTEGRATION**
>
> *BEING: Stay connected to authentic purpose and presence*
>
> *FEELING: Navigate with emotional intelligence and relationship wisdom*
>
> *THINKING: Expand mental models beyond either/or to both/and possibilities*
>
> *DOING: Take action aligned with purpose, building sustainable practices*

This approach required developing what Sirius learned to call "Being Fit For Purpose" – the capacity to serve both community authenticity and professional excellence, to maintain independence whilst engaging productively with government partnerships.

Sirius's refounding journey continues:

➡ *Go to **Section Sirius – PURPOSE – Vantage Point Review** (page 91)*

CAPELLA-3C

When Capella chose to honour her heritage by evolving it rather than just preserving it, she embraced the recognition that their consolidation had created unprecedented opportunity for breakthrough innovation. She gathered her most experienced heritage keepers and most innovative clinical leaders for intensive collaboration sessions focused on "How does our century of caring wisdom become the foundation for approaches that exceed anything the aged care sector has seen?"

"We spent eighteen months proving we could maintain our heritage identity," she told her leadership team, "but I'm realising that wasn't the real challenge. The real opportunity is using our heritage as the platform for clinical innovations that other organisations literally cannot achieve because they don't have our relationship foundation."

The breakthrough came when their longest-serving care manager and newest clinical specialist discovered they were both asking the same question from different angles: "What if excellent clinical care actually requires the relationship wisdom we've developed over a century? What if our heritage isn't something we preserve alongside clinical excellence, but the secret to clinical excellence that feels more human rather than less?"

This insight led to their cross-functional teams that prototyped approaches where century-old caring wisdom informed cutting-edge clinical protocols. Instead of seeing heritage and innovation as separate priorities, they began pioneering breakthrough approaches that could only emerge from their unique combination of relationship expertise and clinical ambition.

The innovation journey led directly to their breakthrough "relationship-informed clinical excellence" model that would transform the aged care sector.

➡ *Continue to **Section Capella – PURPOSE – Vantage Point Review** (page 87)*

POLARIS-3C

When Polaris chose to pursue the innovation that economic pressure had been pointing toward, he reframed their journey from "How do we survive these constraints?" to "What breakthrough approaches do these constraints make necessary for our next evolution?" He convened his leadership team for strategic sessions that treated their economic challenges as innovation catalysts rather than obstacles to manage.

"We've spent two years proving we can maintain financial stability while preserving our values," he told his team, "but I'm realising that wasn't the real achievement we were being called toward. What if these economic conditions are pushing us toward conscious commerce innovations that wouldn't have been necessary under easier circumstances?"

The breakthrough came when their most practical operations manager and most visionary co-founder discovered they were both sensing the same opportunity: "What if my health transformation story and our distributor relationships could become the foundation for approaches that help health-conscious consumers and ethical businesses find each other more effectively? What if we're being called to pioneer the infrastructure for conscious commerce rather than just participate in it?""

This insight led to their innovation teams that prototyped approaches where purpose authenticity became competitive advantage rather than business constraint. Instead of seeing values and market effectiveness as balancing acts, they began pioneering breakthrough approaches that made purpose and profit mutually reinforcing.

The innovation journey led directly to their breakthrough "conscious commerce" model that would influence business education and social enterprise development.

➡ *Continue to* **Section Polaris – PURPOSE alignment – Vantage Point review** *(page 89)*

SIRIUS-3C

When Sirius chose to serve her community better by developing capabilities they hadn't yet explored, she reframed their evolution from "How do we balance authenticity with professional requirements?" to "What would professional excellence look like that actually strengthens our community connections?" She convened working groups that included their most community-rooted members and most professionally skilled volunteers to explore this integration challenge.

"We've spent three years proving we can maintain authentic community relationships while meeting basic professional standards," she told her board, "but I'm realising that wasn't the transformational opportunity we were being offered. What if community authenticity and professional excellence aren't competing priorities, but complementary capacities that strengthen each other when integrated thoughtfully?"

The breakthrough came when their most respected community elder and most qualified professional volunteer discovered they were both envisioning the same possibility: "What if professional standards could be designed from community wisdom rather than imposed on community relationships? What if we could become the bridge that shows both sectors how their approaches enhance rather than compromise each other?"

This insight led to their "Community-Professional Integration Labs" – working groups that prototyped approaches where community authenticity informed professional excellence rather than competing with it. Instead of seeing community connection and professional capability as either/or choices, they began pioneering breakthrough approaches that proved authentic relationships and rigorous standards could be mutually reinforcing.

The innovation journey led directly to their breakthrough "community-informed professional excellence" model that would influence community development policy and government partnership approaches.

➡ *Continue to **Section Sirius – PURPOSE – Vantage Point Review** (page 91)*

CAPELLA – PURPOSE

Vantage Point Review

Three years after choosing the Purpose-Led Transformation Path, Capella leads a network that has become the sector model for "heritage-informed clinical innovation" – care approaches that exceed both traditional relationship standards and contemporary clinical requirements because they integrate rather than choosing between them.

By developing "Being Fit For Purpose" in the beginning stage, Capella discovered that her network's century of caring wisdom could inform breakthrough clinical approaches that newer organisations couldn't achieve because they lacked the relationship foundation that makes clinical care more effective.

The transformation has been remarkable:

Their consolidated network now operates with unified clinical protocols that strengthen rather than compromise relationship quality. Documentation has become a tool for deeper care coordination rather than a barrier to connection. Regulatory compliance emerges from care innovation rather than constraining it. Residents receive clinical care that feels more personal, not less, because relationship expertise informs clinical excellence.

Capella's network is now referenced by regulatory agencies and policy makers as proof that clinical excellence and relationship-centred care are complementary rather than competing priorities. Other aged care organisations seek guidance on "heritage-informed transformation," and Capella mentors leaders throughout the sector on integrating operational consolidation with cultural innovation.

Most significantly, residents and families describe their experience as "clinical care that feels like family" whilst clinical auditors describe it as "relationship-informed excellence." Their approach has influenced aged care policy development and professional training programmes throughout the region.

 YOUR CHOICE DETERMINES YOUR DESTINATION

The Managerial-led Paradigm will make you efficient at managing decline

Purpose-led leadership lifts both the leader and possibilities of what you serve

Which path will you choose?

Capella's leadership has catalysed transformation that extends far beyond her network:

➡ *Go to Section* ***REUNION: Where All Refounding Paths Regroup***

POLARIS – PURPOSE ALIGNMENT

Vantage Point Review

Three years after choosing the Purpose-Led Transformation Path, Polaris leads what has become a model for "conscious commerce" – business approaches that prove purpose authenticity and market effectiveness are mutually reinforcing rather than competing priorities.

By developing "Being Fit For Purpose" in the mid-cycle stage, Polaris discovered that economic constraints could catalyse innovations that strengthen both social impact and business sustainability when approached from abundance rather than scarcity thinking.

The innovation has created breakthrough approaches:

Their distributor relationships now serve values-driven consumers through authentic social impact offerings that competitors can't replicate because they lack the purpose foundation. Their lived experience story has become the cornerstone of product innovations that serve similar families at scale whilst maintaining personal authenticity. Their operations combine efficiency excellence with integrity standards that attract both conscious consumers and ethical investors.

Polaris's company is now studied by business schools and social enterprise networks as proof that purpose-driven approaches can achieve market success that exceeds conventional business models.

Distributors seek partnerships with them because their approach helps retailers serve conscious consumers more effectively than traditional product offerings.

Most remarkably, their team reports feeling more energised than ever because their daily work serves both family impact and business excellence simultaneously. Succession planning has evolved naturally as team members develop leadership capacity through meaningful work that integrates personal values with professional growth.

> **THE PARADIGM CHOICE**
>
> *Managerial-driven decisions focus on protecting against threats rather than creating toward possibilities*
>
> *Purpose-led leadership lifts both the leader and possibilities of what you serve*

Polaris's journey continues as he mentors other mid-cycle purpose-driven business leaders:

➡ *Go to **Section REUNION: Where All Refounding Paths Regroup***

SIRIUS – PURPOSE

Vantage Point Review

Three years after choosing the Purpose-Led Transformation Path, Sirius leads what has become a model for "community-informed professional excellence" – service approaches that prove authentic community connection and professional capability can strengthen rather than compromise each other.

By developing "Being Fit For Purpose" in the renewing/redefining stage, Sirius discovered that government partnerships could enhance rather than constrain their community impact when approached with clear values and innovative integration strategies.

The expansion has created transformative impact:

Their organisation now operates with professional standards that deepen rather than replace authentic community relationships. Government funding supports community-designed programmes rather than bureaucratic service delivery. Their approach has influenced policy development toward community-partnership models that other regions are adapting for their contexts.

Sirius 's organisation is now referenced by government agencies and community development networks as proof that professional excellence and community authenticity can be mutually reinforcing. Other community organisations seek guidance on "values-driven government partnerships," and Sirius mentors leaders on maintaining mission independence whilst engaging productively with institutional funders.

Most significantly, community members describe their experience as "professional services that feel like family" whilst government auditors describe it as "community-informed excellence." Their approach has influenced community development policy and professional training programmes that prioritise relationship alongside competence.

 THE THREE-PHASE JOURNEY

CLARIFY YOUR PATH: Start from purpose and abundance, not problems and scarcity

BE FIT FOR YOUR PATH: Develop integrated wisdom across Being, Feeling, Thinking, and Doing

LIFT YOUR VANTAGE POINT: Purpose-led leadership kindles the spark in others

Sirius's influence continues expanding across community development networks:

➡ *Go to **Section REUNION: Where All Refounding Paths Regroup***

CAPELLA
Vantage Point Review – A

Three years after choosing to preserve heritage approaches without fundamental evolution, Capella leads a network that staff describe as "a place that honours traditional aged care values" and families choose because of their "old-fashioned caring approach."

Capella has become skilled at maintaining relationship-centred care within contemporary regulatory environments. Their network preserves the family atmosphere and caring traditions that distinguish them from more clinical competitors. Staff appreciate working in environments that prioritise human connection, and families value the personal touch that larger corporate providers often lack.

But the deeper challenges that originally required evolution – integrating clinical excellence with relationship care, serving residents with contemporary care needs, developing sustainable approaches for changing aged care realities – remain unaddressed. While they've preserved their heritage identity, they haven't developed the capabilities needed for the clinical intensity that contemporary aged care requires.

Late at night, Capella sometimes wonders what might have been possible if they had embraced heritage as foundation for innovation rather than something to protect from change. Several talented clinical staff have left for organisations pioneering integrated approaches, and she occasionally questions whether heritage preservation was sufficient response to the transformation their sector needed.

> 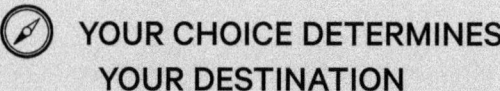 **YOUR CHOICE DETERMINES YOUR DESTINATION**
>
> *The Managerial-led Paradigm will make you efficient at managing decline*
>
> *Purpose-led leadership lifts both the leader and possibilities of what you serve*
>
> **Which path will you choose?**

Capella's network has maintained its heritage character but missed the opportunity for innovation that the consolidation phase could have enabled.

➡ *Go to **Section REUNION: Where All Refounding Paths Regroup***

CAPELLA

Vantage Point Review – B

Three years after choosing systematic integration over breakthrough innovation, Capella leads a network that industry colleagues describe as "a model of steady improvement" and staff appreciate as "a place where heritage and progress work together harmoniously."

Capella has become skilled at managing integrated aged care operations that honour heritage whilst meeting contemporary standards. Their network successfully combines relationship-centred values with clinical competence, achieving regulatory compliance whilst maintaining family atmosphere. The systematic approach has produced consistent improvements across multiple facilities.

But the transformational opportunity that consolidation had created – developing breakthrough approaches that could have positioned them as industry pioneers – remains unrealised. While they've achieved competent integration, they haven't developed the innovative approaches that could have influenced sector transformation. Their network is successful and stable, but not industry-leading.

Late at night, Capella sometimes wonders what might have been possible if they had embraced their consolidation as opportunity for breakthrough innovation rather than systematic improvement. Other networks that took greater risks are now recognised as sector pioneers, while her network is appreciated for steady competence rather than transformational leadership.

> 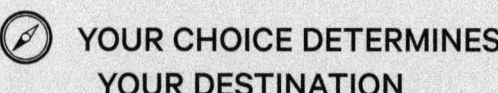 **YOUR CHOICE DETERMINES YOUR DESTINATION**
>
> *The Managerial-led Paradigm will make you efficient at managing decline*
>
> *Purpose-led leadership lifts both the leader and possibilities of what you serve*
>
> **Which path will you choose?**

Capella's network has achieved systematic integration but missed the opportunity for breakthrough innovation that could have transformed their sector.

➡ *Go to* **Section REUNION: Where All Refounding Paths Regroup**

POLARIS

Vantage Point Review – A

Three years after choosing to focus on operational stability rather than innovation-driven growth, Polaris leads a company that employees describe as "a stable place to work with good values" and customers appreciate for "consistent quality and authentic purpose."

Polaris has become skilled at managing a purpose-driven business that balances financial sustainability with values authenticity. Their operations run efficiently, their distributor relationships remain strong, and they've maintained their commitment to integrity and social impact throughout challenging economic conditions.

But the innovation opportunities that economic pressure had revealed – developing breakthrough approaches that could make purpose and profit mutually reinforcing – remain unexplored. While they've achieved operational stability, they haven't developed the growth capabilities needed for the impact scale their purpose could support.

Late at night, Polaris sometimes wonders what might have been possible if they had embraced economic constraints as catalysts for innovation rather than obstacles to manage. Several innovative team members have left for organisations pioneering new approaches, and he occasionally questions whether stability was sufficient response to the evolution their industry needed.

> **KNOW • FOCUS • BE**
>
> *KNOW what matters: Without connection to deeper purpose, efficiency becomes empty activity*
>
> *FOCUS what matters: Trying to serve two paradigms simultaneously serves neither effectively*
>
> *BE what matters: Purpose-led leadership lifts both the leader and possibilities of what you serve*

Polaris's company has achieved financial stability but hasn't developed the innovations that could have amplified their social impact.

➡ *Go to **Section REUNION: Where All Refounding Paths Regroup***

POLARIS

Vantage Point Review – B

Three years after choosing strategic innovation over transformational risk-taking, Polaris leads a company that industry observers describe as "a model of sustainable growth" and employees appreciate as "a place where values and business success work together effectively."

Polaris has become skilled at managing purpose-driven business operations that balance authentic values with market effectiveness. Their company successfully combines integrity standards with operational efficiency, achieving financial sustainability whilst maintaining his health transformation story as authentic foundation. The strategic approach has produced consistent improvements across multiple business metrics.

But the transformational opportunity that economic pressure had revealed – developing breakthrough approaches that could have positioned them as conscious commerce pioneers – remains unrealised. While they've achieved steady improvement, they haven't developed the innovative approaches that could have influenced industry transformation. Their company is successful and stable, but not industry-leading.

Late at night, Polaris sometimes wonders what might have been possible if they had embraced economic constraints as catalysts for breakthrough innovation rather than systematic improvement. Other purpose-driven companies that took greater risks are now recognised as conscious commerce pioneers, while his company is appreciated for steady competence rather than transformational leadership.

> **KNOW • FOCUS • BE**
>
> *KNOW what matters: Without connection to deeper purpose, efficiency becomes empty activity*
>
> *FOCUS what matters: Trying to serve two paradigms simultaneously serves neither effectively*
>
> *BE what matters: Purpose-led leadership lifts both the leader and possibilities of what you serve*

Polaris's company has achieved strategic improvement but missed the opportunity for breakthrough innovation that could have transformed their industry.

➡ *Go to **Section REUNION: Where All Refounding Paths Regroup***

SIRIUS

Vantage Point Review – A

Three years after choosing community authenticity over professional development opportunities, Sirius leads an organisation that members describe as "genuinely community-centred" and volunteers appreciate for "maintaining the personal touch that larger organisations have lost."

Sirius has become skilled at preserving authentic community relationships within contemporary service environments. Their organisation maintains the responsive, relationship-based approaches that distinguish them from more bureaucratic service providers. Members value the personal attention and flexible support that government programmes often can't provide.

But the growth opportunities that government partnerships could have enabled – serving broader populations with enhanced resources whilst maintaining community connection – remain unexplored. While they've preserved their community authenticity, they haven't developed the professional capabilities that could have amplified their service impact.

Late at night, Sirius sometimes wonders what might have been possible if they had embraced professional development as enhancement rather than threat to community connection. Some community members have expressed frustration that needed services are only available through less responsive government programmes, and she occasionally questions whether community purity was sufficient response to the service gaps their organisation could have helped address.

> **THE WISDOM CAPACITIES INTEGRATION**
>
> BEING: Stay connected to authentic purpose and presence
>
> FEELING: Navigate with emotional intelligence and relationship wisdom
>
> THINKING: Expand mental models beyond either/or to both/and possibilities
>
> DOING: Take action aligned with purpose, building sustainable practices

Sirius's organisation has maintained its community character but missed opportunities for expanded impact that values-driven growth could have enabled.

➡ *Go to **Section REUNION: Where All Refounding Paths Regroup***

SIRIUS

Vantage Point Review – B

Three years after choosing strategic partnership over transformational integration, Sirius leads an organisation that sector colleagues describe as "a model of sustainable community development" and members appreciate as "a place where community values and professional standards work together successfully."

Sirius has become skilled at managing community-based organisations that balance authentic relationships with professional capabilities. Their organisation successfully combines community-centred approaches with government partnership requirements, achieving funding security whilst maintaining member satisfaction. The strategic approach has produced consistent improvements across multiple service areas.

But the transformational opportunity that government funding had presented – developing breakthrough approaches that could have positioned them as community-professional integration pioneers – remains unrealised. While they've achieved steady balance, they haven't developed the innovative approaches that could have influenced sector transformation. Their organisation is successful and stable, but not sector-leading.

Late at night, Sirius sometimes wonders what might have been possible if they had embraced funding opportunities as catalysts for breakthrough integration rather than strategic balance. Other community organisations that took greater risks are now recognised as community development pioneers, while her organisation is appreciated for steady competence rather than transformational leadership.

> **THE WISDOM CAPACITIES INTEGRATION**
>
> *BEING: Stay connected to authentic purpose and presence*
>
> *FEELING: Navigate with emotional intelligence and relationship wisdom*
>
> *THINKING: Expand mental models beyond either/or to both/and possibilities*
>
> *DOING: Take action aligned with purpose, building sustainable practices*

Sirius's organisation has achieved strategic balance but missed the opportunity for breakthrough integration that could have transformed their sector.

➡ *Go to* **Section REUNION: Where All Refounding Paths Regroup**

REUNION: WHERE ALL REFOUNDING PATHS REGROUP

Five years after that morning at the crossroads, Capella , Polaris, and Sirius find themselves back at the same campfire – but they're not alone. Leaders from various refounding stages and paths have also returned, drawn by the same questions that had brought them together initially.

FOR PURPOSE LEADERS NAVIGATING WHAT MATTERS

Insightful Pause Practice.

When reviewing the outcomes of your chosen path.

Take time to connect with the wisdom from your journey.

What has this path revealed?

How do these outcomes align with what matters most to me?

What would I carry forward into future choices?

_____

_____

_____

_____

The contrasts are striking, and the conversations reveal patterns that transcend individual organisational experiences.

Leaders who chose managerial-led transformation approaches look professionally accomplished but carry a subtle weariness. They've achieved operational improvements and satisfied stakeholders, but many quietly acknowledge feeling disconnected from the deeper purpose that originally motivated their work. Their organisations are more efficient and stable, but the spark that had ignited their leadership journey feels dimmed.

Leaders who chose purpose-led transformation paths radiate a different kind of energy – not just satisfaction with outcomes, but engagement with ongoing possibility. Their organisations have not only survived transformation but discovered capacities they never knew they possessed. More importantly, they've become catalysts for broader transformation that extends far beyond their organisational boundaries.

The weathered guide appears again, as if she'd been waiting for this convergence of experience and wisdom.

"Each stage teaches essential lessons," she observes, settling beside the rebuilt fire. "The beginning stage builds recognition and courage. The mid-cycle stage develops persistence and integration. The renewing/redefining stage creates influence and legacy."

She pauses, watching the flames flicker across the faces of leaders from different refounding stages and paths.

"But the paradigm choice – managerial-led transformation or purpose-led transformation, constraint or possibility, fear or love – remains constant across all stages. What changes is not the choice itself, but how sophisticated your capacity becomes for embodying that choice in increasingly complex organisational realities."

CROSS-STAGE LEARNING INSIGHTS

As the conversation continues, leaders share insights across refounding stages:

From Beginning Stage Leaders:

- "Recognition often feels risky because it questions approaches that have been successful"
- "Heritage integration requires honouring wisdom whilst pioneering innovation"
- "The scariest part is not knowing what consolidated entities could become together"

From Mid-Cycle Stage Leaders:

- "Economic pressure can catalyse breakthrough innovation when approached from abundance thinking"
- "Succession planning works best when connected to purpose evolution rather than just operational transfer"
- "Maintaining authenticity whilst scaling requires developing new kinds of business wisdom"

From Renewing/Redefining Stage Leaders:

- "Professional excellence and community authenticity can strengthen each other when integrated thoughtfully"

- "Government partnerships become beneficial when approached with clear values and creative integration strategies"
- "The most satisfying aspect is discovering how your organisation's evolution can influence broader sector transformation"

Universal Insights Across All Stages:

- Purpose-led refounding creates more sustainable outcomes than managerial-led improvement
- Each stage creates readiness for deeper transformation at the next level
- Integration thinking (both/and) produces breakthrough approaches that either/or thinking cannot achieve
- The choice between paradigms appears differently at each stage but remains the fundamental decision that determines destination

THE CARE-ECONOMIC REVOLUTION: YOUR CHOICE

As the fire dies down and leaders prepare to continue their journeys, the guide offers final wisdom:

"The Care-Economic Revolution isn't happening somewhere else, in some distant future. It's unfolding right now, through leaders like you who choose to walk the path of purpose rather than just the path of efficiency.

"You've seen tonight that the paradigm choice creates dramatically different outcomes – not just for your organisations, but for the communities you serve, the sectors you influence, and the industries you help transform. The managerial-led paradigm creates efficient organisations that may lose their soul. The purpose-led paradigm creates organisations that strengthen both their impact and their sustainability.

"But here's what you may not have fully realised: **Your choice doesn't just affect your organisation. It affects the entire Care-Economic Revolution.**"

"When you choose purpose-led transformation over managerial-led transformation, possibility over constraint, love over fear – you create ripples that extend far beyond your direct influence. You become proof that another way is possible. You kindle purpose and possibility in others. You contribute to the transformation of how we think about the relationship between care and economics.

"Capella proved that heritage wisdom can inform clinical innovation. Polaris demonstrated that purpose authenticity can enhance market effectiveness. Sirius showed that community connection can strengthen professional excellence. Each of these leaders discovered that the either/or choices they initially faced were actually both/and opportunities for integration.

"The revolution needs your unique gifts, your perspective, your willingness to navigate uncertainty with courage and wisdom. It needs your commitment to integration rather than fragmentation, to collaboration rather than competition, to long-term impact rather than short-term optimisation."

She stands, preparing to leave as dawn breaks over the valley.

"The path is waiting. The choice is yours. But know this: **You are not alone on this journey, and your leadership matters more than you might realise.**"

YOUR NEXT STEPS: CONTINUING THE JOURNEY

As you close this parable and return to your leadership context, you carry with you not just stories and insights, but an invitation to conscious choice about the path forward.

Assess Your Current Stage:

- Are you in the Beginning Stage, integrating heritage wisdom with contemporary capabilities whilst building unified progressive leadership?
- Are you in the Mid-Cycle Stage, using economic pressures and constraints as catalysts for purpose-driven innovations?
- Are you in the Renewing/Redefining Stage, exploring how professional development can strengthen rather than compromise your authentic community connections?

Choose Your Paradigm:

- Will you approach your challenges from managerial-led transformation thinking (fear-based, scarcity-oriented, problem-focused) or purpose-led transformation thinking (love-based, abundance-oriented, possibility-focused)?
- Will you optimise within current constraints or transform the constraints themselves into opportunities for breakthrough innovation?

- Will you choose between competing priorities or pioneer integration approaches that serve multiple values simultaneously?

Take Your Next Step: Your refounding journey continues with every choice you make. The terrain varies by stage, but the destination – becoming an organisation that kindles purpose and possibility whilst creating sustainable impact – remains constant throughout the journey.

BEING FIT FOR PURPOSE: THE COMPREHENSIVE GUIDE

The stories you've just experienced represent real patterns observed across hundreds of purpose-led organisations. The frameworks, practices, and approaches that support this transformation are detailed in our comprehensive guide: **"Kindling Purpose Leaders: How To Lead Through The Care-Economic Revolution."**

This companion guide provides:

For Beginning Stage Leaders:

- Heritage integration frameworks for honouring wisdom whilst pioneering innovation
- Tools for building unified leadership across consolidated organisations
- Assessment approaches for clinical-relationship capability development
- Strategies for engaging stakeholders in conscious evolution that transcends either/or choices

For Mid-Cycle Stage Leaders:

- Innovation frameworks for using economic pressure as catalyst for breakthrough approaches
- Succession planning tools that connect leadership development with purpose evolution

- Methods for scaling authenticity without compromising values foundation
- Approaches for maximising existing relationships whilst developing new capabilities

For Renewing/Redefining Stage Leaders:

- Professional development frameworks that strengthen community authenticity
- Partnership strategies for engaging government funding whilst maintaining mission independence
- Tools for evolving member engagement across generational and cultural changes
- Models for expanding impact whilst preserving responsive, relationship-based approaches

Integrated Across All Stages:

- The Wisdom Capacity Integration Practice™
- Purpose-Led vs Managerial-Led Paradigm Assessment
- Trail Markers for navigation across terrain difficulty
- Both/And Integration Tools for transcending either/or limitations

THE TRAIL MARKERS

Essential Wisdom for Purpose-Led Leaders

As you continue your journey, keep these insights visible to guide your navigation:

THE PARADIGM CHOICE

Managerial-driven decisions focus on protecting against threats rather than creating toward possibilities

Purpose-led leadership lifts both the leader and possibilities of what you serve

Care-Economic Crunch *Managerial-Led Paradigm*	Care-Economic Revolution *Purpose-Led Paradigm*
Fear	Love
Judgement	Discernment
Blame (outside in)	Responsibility (inside out)
Passive / Powerless	Intention / Co-Creator
Focus on circle of concern & what you can't fix	Focus on the circle of influence & grow impact
Seeing a problem	Seeing an opportunity
Short Term	Short & Long Term
My success (individualistic)	Impact greater than self (collective)
Dependant and independant	Independant & Interdependant
Seeing parts / issues	Seeing interconnectedness
Limited & self-preservation	Abundant & generous

KNOW • FOCUS • BE

KNOW what matters: Without connection to deeper purpose, efficiency becomes empty activity

FOCUS what matters: Trying to serve two paradigms simultaneously serves neither effectively

BE what matters: Purpose-led leadership lifts both the leader and possibilities of what you serve

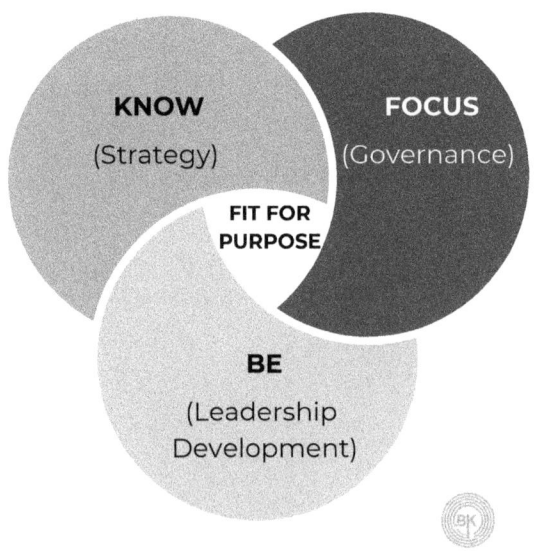

FOR PURPOSE LEADERS NAVIGATING WHAT MATTERS

THE THREE-PHASE JOURNEY

CLARIFY YOUR PATH: Start from purpose and abundance, not problems and scarcity

BE FIT FOR YOUR PATH: Develop integrated wisdom across Being, Feeling, Thinking, and Doing

LIFT YOUR VANTAGE POINT: Purpose-led leadership kindles the spark in others

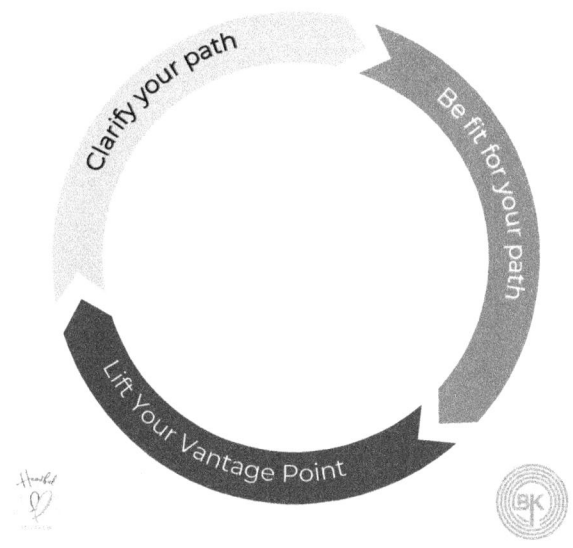

THE WISDOM CAPACITIES INTEGRATION

BEING: Stay connected to authentic purpose and presence

FEELING: Navigate with emotional intelligence and relationship wisdom

THINKING: Expand mental models beyond either/or to both/and possibilities

DOING: Take action aligned with purpose, building sustainable practices

WISDOM CAPACITIES INTEGRATION™

Triple Loop Learning and Leading - Expanding Organisational Wisdom

1. Following the Maps
2. Questioning the Maps
3. Creating New Maps

FOR PURPOSE LEADERS NAVIGATING WHAT MATTERS

 YOUR CHOICE DETERMINES YOUR DESTINATION

The Managerial-led Paradigm will make you efficient at managing decline

Purpose-led leadership lifts both the leader and possibilities of what you serve

Which path will you choose?

PurposeOrgOS™
For your trek ahead.
For your next strategic cycle.

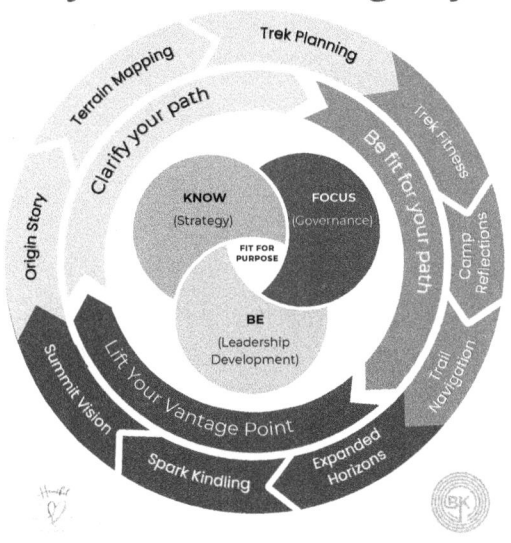

> Your refounding adventure continues with every choice you make. The terrain varies by stage, but the destination – becoming an organisation that kindles purpose and possibility whilst creating sustainable impact – remains constant across the entire journey.
>
> The choice, as always, is yours to make.
>
> But you don't have to make it alone.

This parable was created for purpose-led leaders navigating the Care-Economic Revolution. It represents patterns observed across thousands of organisations and leaders who have chosen to walk the path of conscious organisational evolution.

For more resources, tools, and community support for your refounding journey, visit www.PurposeOrgOS.com to access your free Trek Readiness Mini-Kit and connect with other purpose-led leaders.

Your adventure in creating organisations that serve both care and economics continues with every choice you make.

A BIT ABOUT BERNIE & VEE

Bernie Kelly, Co-Founder, PurposeOrgOS

My journey is shaped by an obsession with helping purpose-led leaders remain "fit for purpose" as the strategic environment shifts around them. When I reflect I see the deep roots of interconnected family and growing up in a rural community that continues to work and evolve together. Through decades of working with leaders who choose to be leaders rather than observers from health and aged care to professional services and manufacturing I discovered that the most transformative leaders don't just solve their own organisational challenges, they kindle sparks that ignite positive change throughout their entire ecosystem. This is the foundation of my work: creating world-class resources and tailor-made spaces where purpose-led leaders develop the strategic momentum to transform not just their organisations, but their industries – proving that individual transformation creates ripple effects that shape a better world.

https://www.linkedin.com/in/berniekelly100/

Vee Haslam, Co-Founder, PurposeOrgOS

Being aligned with our purpose is not just important to ourselves, our organisations and those we work around, but I also strongly believe it is integral to our world and the legacy we want to co-create for future generations. I have found myself on an unfolding quest to be connected with my own purpose and to stay on the path. As well as having the blessing of supporting many purpose-driven individuals and teams who want to make a positive difference in our world. Through this experience over the past couple of decades, I have found that truly impactful leaders are those who remain present to challenge – allowing complexity, emotion, and insight to coexist. Sustainable transformation happens when leaders reconnect with their essence and honour the human experience as a source of power, not a problem to fix. This became the foundation of my ever-evolving contribution: creating presence-based tools and Mojo practices where leaders return to the heart of the matter – in service of co-creating a corporate paradigm where we share our unique gifts for an abundant world for all.

https://www.linkedin.com/in/team-collaboration-transformation-melbourne/

PurposeOrgOS™

For your trek ahead. For your next strategic cycle.

Refounding Purpose-Driven Organisations for What Matters Now and Next

Is This You?

"Our organisation was built on purpose. But lately… something's off."

You might not have the words yet. But your team feels it.

- You're working harder – yet more disconnected
- Growth is increasing – but alignment is dispersing
- You know the way forward isn't through old systems – it's through something deeper

Why PurposeOrgOS™ Matters Now

Our world needs organisations with heart more than ever. While traditional leadership approaches are fragmenting the very organisations we need most – those built on care, purpose, and human connection. We created PurposeOrgOS™ because *Fit For Purpose* organisations aren't just good business – they're essential for our abundant world for all. We must change how we lead to ensure these vital organisations don't just survive, but thrive and transform our collective future.

Built For:

- Purpose-first organisations ($10M–$1B)
- Care sector leaders navigating complexity
- Leadership teams preparing for strategic shifts
- Organisations choosing between authenticity and growth

PurposeOrgOS™:

Your Organisational Operating System For what matters now and next, helping you:

- Refound your organisation without losing what you've built
- Navigate complexity with leadership frameworks that match this moment
- Realign teams, strategy, and decision-making with your deepest purpose
- Lead the Care-Economic Revolution, where growth and care strengthen each other

Ready for Your Trek?

- Take the Diagnostic – Map your Trek Terrain level
- Choose Your Path – Solo, Guided, or Summit engagement
- Activate the OS – Transform your team from the inside out
- Lead from the New – Refound your purpose organisation

You're not starting over. You're refounding.

Let PurposeOrgOS™ help you bring viability and vitality back to your organisation so you evolve without losing the heart of what you stand for.

Learn more: www.PurposeOrgOS.com